Contents

Any words appearing in bold, **like this**, are explained in the Glossary.

Soil and its properties

All the things we use are made from materials. Soil is a material. It is made from a mixture of many different materials. Much of the Earth's surface is covered with soil. Plants need soil to grow and it provides a home for many different creatures.

Humans use soil too. We need it for growing crops, for making buildings and for many other things.

Trees cannot live without soil.

How We Use

Soil

Carol Ballard

www.raintreepublishers.co.uk

Visit our website to find out more information about **Raintree** books.

To order:

☎ Phone 44 (0) 1865 888112

▤ Send a fax to 44 (0) 1865 314091

▢ Visit the Raintree bookshop at **www.raintreepublishers.co.uk** to browse our catalogue and order online.

First published in Great Britain by Raintree,
Halley Court, Jordan Hill, Oxford OX2 8EJ,
part of Harcourt Education.
Raintree is a registered trademark of Harcourt
Education Ltd.

Editorial: Nick Hunter and Richard Woodham
Design: Kim Saar and Bridge Creative Services Ltd
Picture Research: Maria Joannou and Debra Weatherley
Production: Amanda Meaden
Indexing: Indexing Specialists (UK) Ltd

Originated by Ambassador Litho Ltd
Printed and bound in Hong Kong, China by
South China Printing Company

ISBN 1 844 43440 0
09 08 07 06 05
10 9 8 7 6 5 4 3 2 1

British Library Cataloguing in Publication Data
Ballard, Carol
How We Use Soil. – (Using Materials)
620.1'91
A full catalogue record for this book is available from
the British Library.

Acknowledgements
The publishers would like to thank the following for
permission to reproduce photographs: Alamy pp. **8**
(ImageState/Neil McIntyre), **13** (Plainpicture/T.
Grimm), **19** (Eric Smith), **20** (Harcourt Index); Art
Directors & Trip p. **25**; Corbis p. **4**; Ecoscene pp. **9, 14,
28** (Taxi); Garden Picture Library p. **21** (Stone); Getty
Images pp. **5** (Stone), **10** (Stone), **17** (Photographers
Choice), **23** (Paul Kay), **27** (Bruce Herrod); Oxford
Scientific Films pp. **6, 15** (Steve Turner), **18** (David
Scharf), **22** (Lynwood Chace); Science Photo Library
pp. **7** (Jeremy Walker), **12** (Dr. Jeremy Burgess), **16**
(Andrew Syred), **24** (Dr. Jeremy Burgess), **26, 29**;
Tudor Photography p. **11**.

Cover photograph of a potter producing clay oil lights
for Diwali Festival, Madhya Pradesh, India, reproduced
with permission of Thirdangle.

Every effort has been made to contact copyright
holders of any material reproduced in this book. Any
omissions will be rectified in subsequent printings if
notice is given to the publishers.

The paper used to print this book comes from
sustainable resources.

Soil is home to many living creatures, such as this mole.

The **properties** of a material tell us what it is like. The properties of soil make it a good material to use for certain jobs. It contains everything that plants need to grow. It can be moulded into shapes and some soils can be baked to make them strong. It is also crumbly so it can be moved easily.

Don't use it!
The different properties of materials make them useful for some jobs. The properties also make them unsuitable for other jobs. For example, we don't normally use soil to make containers for water. Soil is not **waterproof***.*

What is soil made from?

Soil is a **natural** material. It is a mixture of many different things. The rocks that make up the surface of the Earth are being worn away by wind and rain all the time. Tiny pieces break off these rocks and become part of the soil. When plants and animals die, they are slowly broken down into very small pieces. This dead material also becomes part of the soil.

Soil may change colour as you dig deeper.

This is a close-up of a type of micro-organism called a nematode.

Soil contains **micro-organisms**. These are living things that are too small to be seen without a **microscope**. Larger animals such as beetles, worms and ants crawl around in the soil too. Soil also contains water and air, which are important for everything that lives there.

Looking at soil

If soil is mixed with water and shaken, the water becomes a dull brown. If it is left for a while, the water will clear and you can see different layers of soil collecting at the bottom. This lets you see some of the different materials that soil is made from.

What is soil like?

To explain what soil is like, we need to think about what it looks and feels like. Soil is usually a shade of brown. Some soils are a very dark, blackish brown. Others are very pale. Soils look different because they are made from different mixtures of materials.

The soil where these grapes are growing contains lots of chalk. This makes it look very pale.

How would you describe the soil in your garden or school grounds?

If you rub some soil between your fingers, you will find out what it feels like. This is called its **texture**. Some soils are very crumbly, especially when they are dry. Some are chalky, while others are sandy. Some soils are sticky when they are wet and very hard when they are dry. These different **properties** mean that different soils are useful for different jobs.

Soil for writing

If the ground under the soil is a pale white colour, the soil may contain pieces of chalk. If you rub chalk across a hard, dark surface you will make a white line.

Soil and drainage

When water touches soil, it starts to soak in between the tiny pieces that make up the soil. It works its way through the soil and on to whatever lies beneath. It then drains away, just like your bathwater does when you pull out the plug.

This process is called **drainage**. If soil contains a lot of stones or sand, water will drain away very quickly. These soils soon dry out. Sandy soil can be added to **bogs** to improve their drainage.

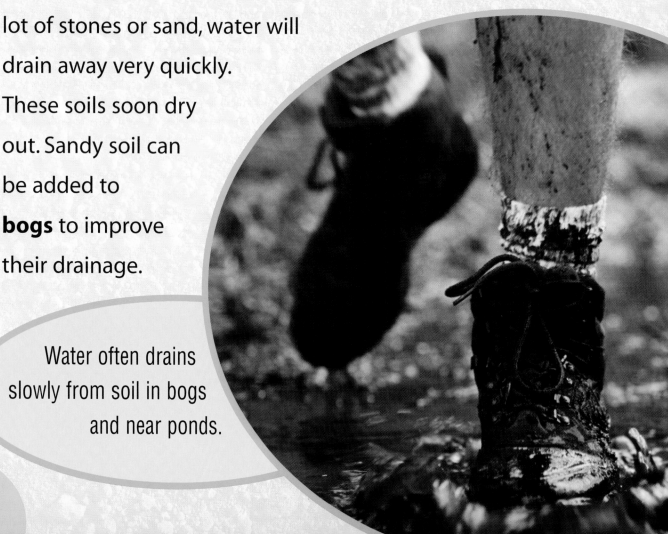

Water often drains slowly from soil in bogs and near ponds.

You could test soils from different places to see whether some drain more quickly than others do.

Some soils, like those with a lot of sticky clay, let water drain away very slowly. They stay damp for a long time. Some plants and animals can only live in areas where the soil stays damp.

Don't use it!

*We don't build swimming pools and large garden ponds by just digging holes in the soil. They need to be lined with a **waterproof** material such as plastic or concrete so the water does not drain away.*

Soil for growing

Soil is soft and crumbly. This means that plant roots can grow down into the soil. Some plants have roots that spread out over a wide area. Others have roots that grow deep down into the ground.

Soil holds the plant's roots firmly in place and stops the plant from being blown away by a strong wind or washed away by water.

These tiny roots will soon grow big and strong.

Each of these plants started life as a tiny seed in the soil.

If you put some kitchen towel on a pool of water, the water is **absorbed** by it. Water from the soil is absorbed by plant roots in the same way. The water is then carried to the parts of the plant that need it. **Minerals** from the soil are also absorbed by the roots. Plants need minerals to grow strong and to stay healthy.

Adding extras...

*Gardeners often add things to the soil to help their plants grow. Some use **compost**. Others use special mixtures of **chemicals** called **fertilizers**. These all make the soil rich and fertile, so that the plants have everything they need to grow well.*

13

How plants use soil

Many plants grow from seeds. Some people sow seeds in special trays and pots. Some seeds can be scattered straight on to the ground. In nature, seeds are spread around in many ways, but unless they land on soil they are unlikely to grow.

Did you know that potatoes grow under the ground?

These roots should be under the soil – but the wind was too strong for this tree.

A tiny root pushes out of the seed's case and grows down into the soil. A shoot grows upwards and tiny leaves appear on it. The roots **absorb** water and **minerals** from the soil, which help the plant to grow. The roots grow longer to provide support for the plant. Many plants have flowers that make seeds. When these seeds land on the soil, the process starts again.

Different types of soil

Soil is not the same everywhere. In some places, the soil has everything that plants need to grow well and the land looks green and rich. In other places, the soil does not have everything that plants need. Most plants that grow in these places are not as strong or healthy, and the land is more bare.

Soil for farming

Farmers grow crops such as wheat and corn that we use to make bread. They also grow vegetables such as potatoes and carrots, and fruits such as apples and strawberries. All of these crops need soil to grow.

The farmer has to plough the soil before any seeds can be planted. Soil can be ploughed because it is soft. The farmer may spread **fertilizer** on the soil so that there are plenty of **nutrients** to help the crops grow well.

Ploughing the soil helps to get it ready for planting seeds.

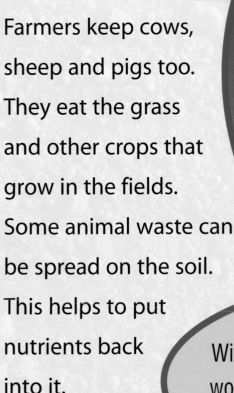

Farmers keep cows, sheep and pigs too. They eat the grass and other crops that grow in the fields. Some animal waste can be spread on the soil. This helps to put nutrients back into it.

Without soil, there would be no grass for cows to eat – so we would have no milk!

Don't use it!

Different plants need different nutrients. Farmers try not to plant the same crop in one field year after year. Sometimes they leave a field without a crop for a year. This gives the soil time to recover and allows the nutrients that the plants have used to be replaced.

Soil for living in

Soil is home to many creatures. Some, like **bacteria** and **fungi**, are **micro-organisms**. Ants and mites are still very small but can be seen without a **microscope**. Slugs, snails, centipedes and beetles also live in the soil. The soil contains water and air spaces that help all these creatures to live. Some eat dead plant and animal material. Some are pests and eat plant roots.

Snails lay eggs in the soil. The eggs hatch out into baby snails.

Larger animals also live in the soil. Moles spend their lives underground. They can tunnel through the crumbly soil. Rabbits dig holes in the soil to sleep in but come out above the ground to feed.

Helpful worms

Earthworms are good for the soil. They drag dead leaves and other materials into the soil and help to break them down. As they tunnel through the soil, they make spaces that let air in and help water to drain away.

Rabbits have strong front legs and paws that help them to dig tunnels.

Soil for rotting

When plants and animals die, they rot. This means that they slowly break down. All the **chemicals** that they were made of go back into the soil. The chemicals can then be used by plants to grow. If nothing rotted, dead plants and animals would just pile up on the ground.

As these apples rot, the chemicals that made them will go back into the soil.

This compost heap helps a gardener to **recycle** things like dead plants and vegetable peelings.

Dead material cannot rot on its own. It has to be attacked by **micro-organisms** such as **bacteria** and **fungi**. These micro-organisms like warm, damp places. Soil contains lots of micro-organisms.

Rotten vegetables!

*Many people have **compost** heaps in their gardens. They put vegetable peelings and other plant material in them. When they rot, compost is produced. This is full of the **nutrients** that plants need to grow. Gardeners spread compost around their gardens to feed their plants.*

Soil for building

Many buildings are made from bricks. Bricks are made from soil. The best soil for making bricks is clay. This is sticky when it is wet but when it dries it becomes hard and strong. The clay can be pressed into a mould to make it into the right shape. The bricks are then left to dry in the air.

Bricks can be made in all sorts of different shapes, colours and sizes.

This mud hut in Utah, USA, has been made using soil and a wooden frame.

Once dry, the bricks have to be heated to make them harden. To do this, the bricks are put into a big oven called a kiln and heated to a very high temperature. The bricks are then taken out of the kiln and left to cool. They are now ready to be used.

Don't use it!
Bricks cannot be used for all the parts of a building. We don't use bricks to make window frames. Materials such as wood or metal are lighter or stronger so we use these instead.

Moving soil

Sometimes, soil needs to be moved. Gardeners move soil when they want to plant a new flowerbed. They can use a spade to move these small amounts of soil. Huge amounts of soil often need to be moved when new roads or houses are built. Large machines called **excavators** are used for jobs like this.

It would take a long time to move this much soil without an excavator!

This river has moved soil to carve out all these twists and turns.

Soil is much easier to move than rocks. It can be moved in big loads or small loads. Banks of soil are built beside rivers. They stop the rivers flooding. Soil can also be made flat so that new roads can be laid.

Rivers move soil!

*If a river flows quickly, it takes soil out of the river banks. As the river gets bigger and slows down, the soil is dropped. Over many years this can change the shape of a river's course. Lots of **nutrients** from the river are also left so the soil becomes rich and fertile.*

Changing soil

Soil is always changing. As plants grow, they use **nutrients** from the soil. When they die, they rot and the nutrients are returned to the soil. The animals that live in the soil die too. Their bodies are broken down and become part of the soil. The nutrients can be used again. We need soil to keep changing so that it contains all the nutrients that plants need to grow .

This is a soil mite, a **micro-organism** that breaks down dead plants.

Pieces of rock broken off by this stream may be carried long distances by the water.

The small stones and tiny pieces of rock that are found in soil come from much bigger rocks. These large rocks have been worn away over time by wind and rain. Small pieces have been broken off and carried away by streams. They are left behind as the water flows along and become mixed into the soil.

Changing with the weather

Changes in the weather cause changes in the soil. A lot of heavy rain fills the spaces in the soil with water. It becomes wet and squelchy. In hot, dry weather the soil becomes hard. Big cracks appear in it.

Soil and the environment

Soil plays an important part in our **environment**. It affects plants, animals and humans. Heavy rain can **erode** soil. The water loosens the soil as it drains away. Cutting down trees makes this problem worse. Tree roots can help to hold the soil in place and stop it from being washed away.

A forest grew here once but now the trees have all been cut down.

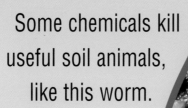
Some chemicals kill useful soil animals, like this worm.

Heavy rain on hills can cause a landslide. This can damage buildings and hurt any people, animals or plants that get in its way. The soil from the hill is deposited in a new place. If there is a river at the bottom of the hill, the soil may block it.

Poisoning soil

*Many farmers have used **chemicals** to kill weeds and pests. These help their crops to grow, but the chemicals can stay in the soil for many years. They can be washed into lakes and rivers where they may harm people and animals. Many of these chemicals are now **illegal** in many countries.*

Find out for yourself

The best way to find out more about soil is to investigate it for yourself. Look around for soil being used, and keep an eye out for soil during your day. You will find the answers to many of your questions in this book. You can also look in other books and on the Internet.

Books to read

Rocks and Minerals: Soil, Melissa Stewart (Heinemann Library, 2002)

Step by Step Geography: Farming and Industry, Patience Coster (Franklin Watts, 2000)

Using the Internet

Try searching the Internet to find out about soil. Websites can change, so if some of the links below no longer work, don't worry. Use a search engine such as www.yahooligans.com or www.internet4kids.com. You could try searching using the keywords 'compost', 'landslide' and 'crop farming'. Here are some websites to get you started.

Websites

A great site, which explains all about different materials: http://www.bbc.co.uk/schools/revisewise/science/materials/

Soil-related news, information and activities: http://ltpwww.gsfc.nasa.gov/globe/index.htm

Glossary

absorb soak up liquid

bacteria type of micro-organism

bog place that stays damp and soggy

chemical substance that we use to make other substances, or for jobs such as cleaning

compost rotting plant and animal material used to add nutrients to soil

drainage letting water pass through

environment world around us

erode wear away rocks or soil

excavator large machine used for moving heavy things

fertilizer chemicals that help plants to grow

fungi name given to a group of plants which includes mushrooms and some moulds

illegal against the law

micro-organism living thing that is so small it can only be seen with a microscope

microscope instrument used for looking closely at things

minerals chemicals that plants need

natural anything that is not made by people

nutrients parts of food needed by living things for energy and growth

property characteristic or quality of a material

recycle use again

texture how something feels, such as rough, smooth or shiny

waterproof material that does not let water pass through it

Index

Titles in the *Using Materials* series include:

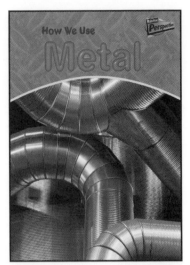

Hardback   1 844 43436 2

Hardback   1 844 43437 0

Hardback   1 844 43438 9

Hardback   1 844 43439 7

Hardback   1 844 43440 0

Hardback   1 844 43441 9

Find out about the other titles in this series on our website www.raintreepublishers.co.uk